There are so many responsibilities ___ _____ ___ _____
the task can seem overwhelming. Lee Danesco's practical, how-to guide not
only eases the anxiety over these, but also expands the creative and joyful
possibilities inherent in the role.

✦ **KATHY HENDRICKS**, *workshop presenter and author of*
   Everything about Parish Ministry I Wish I Had Known

If you are excited about sharing the Catholic faith with future generations,
then ***Here's How: A Catechist's Guide*** is a necessary resource for
you! With twenty-four years of experience working with both teachers and
students, Lee Danesco offers valuable support and practical tips for the
classroom that will appeal to both the beginning volunteer and the veteran
catechist. This book will help catechists understand what is expected of
them, how to prepare a successful lesson, and simple ways to motivate
students. From detailed classroom activities to ideas for working with
parents, this book is a must-have for every catechist.

✦ **ROBYN LEE**, *Editor,*
   RTJ's Creative Catechist

Lee Danesco's *Here's How* encourages catechists to trust themselves, while
it offers them advice about being precise and fearless in learning what they
do not know. Lee proposes a clear design on how best to engage young
people in the learning experience. From offering ways to incorporate the
arts, to understanding discipline, to encouraging developing conversation
skills, this book complements parish catechetical formation. The parish
catechetical leader will find it an invaluable tool.

✦ **SUSAN J. KAY**, *Assistant Director of Religious Education/*
   Catechetical Leadership, Archdiocese of Boston

Lee Danesco draws on more than twenty-four years of experience when she
says "here's how"...to prepare, motivate, evaluate, maximize time, use small
group activities, and get help. Her practical ideas give catechists—both the
rookie and the veteran—the tools that will help them be confident in the
classroom, realistic about expectations, focused on the tasks, and effective
in the mission of sharing their Catholic faith with their students.

✦ **KASS DOTTERWEICH**, *Editor,*
   Catechist

Lee offers an informative, practical, must-read for catechists of all levels; from first-year to the most seasoned. Her detailed, organized, ingenious style leads the reader on a walk through a religious education class while she offers sound advice on planning, presentation, methods, and summary. Parishes would certainly be offering their catechists an invaluable service by providing them with their very own copy.

ͦ **CATHY O'CONNELL**, *Religious Education Director,*
   St. Jude's Parish, Norfolk, MA

Here's How: A Catechist's Guide is full of very practical information for every catechist. Motivating students to be excited about their faith is not an easy task. Lee has clearly outlined many ideas that truly work. This book is a must for every religious education office!

ͦ **KAREN ACKLES**, *Religious Education Director,*
   St Mary Parish, Franklin, MA

Here's How is a masterpiece! It has everything we need for practical and meaningful teaching. It is insightful and inspiring, with a wealth of methodology that is sure to guide catechists on their journey to teach as Christ taught.

ͦ **SHARON GUERIN**, *Religious Education Director,*
   St. Martha Parish, Plainville, MA

The ESSENTIAL CATECHIST'S BOOKSHELF

Here's How

A Catechist's Guide

Planning and Teaching Your Catechetical Sessions

Lee Danesco

Dedication

To Sarah, Ben, Lexi, Jake, and Ryan,
for the inspiration of all their
"how" questions

TWENTY-THIRD PUBLICATIONS
1 Montauk Avenue, Suite 200, New London, CT 06320
(860) 437-3012 » (800) 321-0411 » www.23rdpublications.com

ISBN: 978-1-62785-011-7
Library of Congress Catalog Card Number: 2013957106
Printed in the U.S.A.

Contents

INTRODUCTION

Chances are that prayer, the sacraments, Mass, Scripture, and Christian service are already part of your life. In your own way and without setting out to do so, you effectively model what it means to be a practicing Catholic. You're excited about becoming a catechist and you should be. You have lots to offer.

Still, in the back of your mind, some doubts have slowly formed around a small but provocative word— "how." In odd moments you may wonder:

How will I connect with a room full of children?

How will I teach for a full sixty minutes?

How will I manage small-group activities?

How will I know if I am reaching my students or not?

The list goes on but the theme remains the same: "How will I suddenly become a 'teacher' when I have never taught before?"

While not claiming to have all the answers, *Here's How* addresses common problems faced by anyone who has ever stepped up to teach children. Meeting you at teaching junctures where you are most likely to struggle, *Here's How* offers support and practical solutions that can help you cross the divide between living the faith and teaching it.

Drawing on twenty-four years of experience working with both teachers and students, the author invites you to replace "How?" with "Here's how."

How to weigh expectations

Good for you. You heard the annual request for volunteer teachers and this year decided to say "yes." But since that moment of commitment, have you been wondering just exactly what you signed on to do?

Reviewing what is expected of the typical volunteer catechist can help you fill in the blanks by replacing wondering with understanding. The reality checklist that follows is meant to give you the focus and direction you need as you prepare to serve as a parish catechist.

WHAT'S EXPECTED OF YOU

Have a plan
When the first day of class arrives, you will be asked to take charge of a small group of children, in a designated learning space, to share an assigned lesson. Amidst whatever distractions or confusion that first meeting presents, the Director of Religious Education (DRE), students, and parents will expect

you to be prepared and ready to teach. You'll be expected to have a plan.

No matter the grade level, the class size, or the lesson content, every class you teach requires basic, commonsense planning. There is no escaping that chore. Planning is the pivot around which every lesson revolves.

In fact, planning is so important that well in advance of the first class meetings, DREs routinely gather volunteer catechists to lay the groundwork for the teaching year ahead.

At that meeting, or before your first class, you should receive a catechist's guide and instructions on its use. Skimming through the guide, you'll note that a sizeable portion of the weekly lesson planning has already been done for you. The guide logically divides the year's work into teaching topics arranged by chapters. Then each chapter is broken down into distinct blocks of related subject matter with accompanying activities geared to fill the teaching hour.

With so much of the planning completed, it's fair to ask what is left for you to do.

The answer: attend that organizational meeting and make the pre-structured guide material your own. The meeting ideally provides the perfect format in which to review weekly teaching plans, become familiar with lesson highlights, and share outstanding problems or concerns. Catechists' meetings can effectively raise your level of teaching readiness. You should leave the meeting supported by clear-cut directions for successfully completing your first lesson and a pattern for planning the rest.

Even if your parish does not offer this initial planning session, don't worry. You will find detailed information and explanations of lesson planning and preparation in Chapter 3: How to Teach Well for Sixty Minutes, and Chapter 4: How to Motivate Students.

Value each child

A positive, fair, and caring approach toward each individual student stands high on any list of what parents, students, and DREs will expect from you as a catechist.

While it sounds simple enough, the process of valuing a child takes in a good deal of territory. It includes the expectation that even in the middle of group-centered activities, crafts, or games, you will work to remain conscious of and attuned to the particular needs, challenges, and sensitivities of each individual student no matter how well masked they may be.

Accepting the challenge to value students as individuals means going well beyond simply short-circuiting the thoughtless and potentially hurtful words and actions of young people toward one another. As the catechist, you are charged with creating and maintaining the kind of classroom atmosphere in which all children can routinely feel safe and secure enough to learn and grow according to their God-given gifts.

The entire parish community, but especially parents, will count on you to insist that students in your classroom will learn to value one another as God's cherished children, and that the Christian attitude of love toward one another will prevail.

Be relevant to student grade level

With equal intensity, but for very different reasons, both your students and the DRE are hoping that you will begin the year motivated to teach lessons mindful of the age group you are teaching.

Children respond best when catechists use approaches, activities, language, and even humor that are tailored just for them. They are quickly turned off by classroom experiences in which the adult in charge speaks to them without eye contact or connection, even if unintentionally. While students don't require the presence of a three-ring circus to get and hold their attention, they do prefer that you structure lessons to share "with" them, not teach "at" them. Students don't want to feel bored, left out, or invisible in their own learning space. Your decision to teach from a mindset that welcomes student ideas, opinions, and participation can make all the difference. Students look for you to make teaching choices that are in their favor.

From the DRE's perspective, you won't be expected to arrive at the first class fully adjusted to the grade level you are about to teach. But she or he will want you to recognize the value of working toward accommodating that particular level of learners as you teach from week to week.

That's because DREs know that even your best-prepared lesson plan is likely to fall short if you fail to create rapport with your students. You don't need to take a crash course in child psychology to connect with young people, but you do need to find ways to get to know, understand, and give a feeling of comfort to your students.

Just as the religion textbook is designed to match the reading and comprehension level of your students, so your instructive stories, examples, and activities should take into account who they are and the environment that surrounds them.

Don't worry about memorizing the names of their favorite movies, songs, or heroes, but do give attention and respect to the important place those things occupy in their lives at the moment. DREs will expect you to meet children where they are because DREs know connection is a powerful first step toward engaging children in almost any lesson pursuit.

Discipline

Successful teaching requires classroom discipline. This is an axiom that experience makes difficult to dispute.

Discipline is such a crucial aspect of the total religious education program that parish leadership, including the DRE, generally assumes the ultimate responsibility for generating program-wide regulations.

It's not likely, then, that you will be asked to construct a far-reaching disciplinary code for your class. Still, it will be left to you to put in place a few commonsense rules that promote classroom order and reasonable noise levels.

Regardless of the total number or substance of rules in play, everyone from the youngest student to the most senior parishioner will expect you, as a catechist, to take an active role in enforcing standards that allow for safe and productive religious education.

Model the faith

While they might not discuss it with you very often, parents, the DRE, and children really do see each catechist as a potential faith model for students. That is why such care is given to the selection and assignment of volunteers. You are taking on a position of great trust. You are expected to model the faith for children.

Fortunately, parents and the DRE also have a realistic take on catechists. They know and respect the fact that you are neither a professional teacher nor a canonized saint. They won't ask you to be either. What they will ask is that you recognize the visible link between teaching and living the faith.

Parents expect that you will do your best to help their children explore the faith through books, crafts, games, and activities. But they also know that, beyond the lesson, other less apparent learning is going on as well. They believe their children will learn a great lesson about how Catholic Christians live the faith through simple observation. They are counting on you to provide one trustworthy model. When it comes to placing demands on catechists, children can be a remarkably lenient crowd. They won't mind so much if you skip a teaching point or lose your place in a story. They'll understand if you are a bit out of sorts or less patient than usual. They'll even be okay if sometimes your actions don't precisely mirror what you have been teaching. But you need to know: they will notice.

They won't expect you to be perfect, but they will expect you to give regular evidence of trying hard to live as a practicing Christian.

Be yourself

The catechist's guide you receive will provide you with a lesson plan and some general directions to get you started. To make the best use of those aids, you will be encouraged to use your own special collection of abilities and strengths. Yes, the DRE will expect you to stay on message, but he or she will also allow you room to broaden the appeal of a topic or make it more comprehensible to students by injecting a bit of yourself into the lesson.

Every catechist at your grade level will be teaching from precisely the same catechist's guide and conducting the same lesson, but no two catechists will share the lesson in exactly the same way. Nor should they. That's because each teacher is expected to energize each lesson through the use of his or her particular gift set. Your honest rendition of a lesson cannot help but add a personal tone and memorable twist to every lesson you share.

Each week you'll be expected to teach a unique lesson because as you teach you will be expected to be yourself.

SUMMARY

If all this sounds a little daunting, you may want to add just a touch of perspective:

1. You need to have a plan, but only for one hour at a time, and the catechist's guide has already done half the work for you.

2. Yes, value each child, but, honestly, how many children are we talking about—a dozen or less?

3. Teach at grade level, but only one grade level needs to be mastered.

4. Discipline is a must, but, again, the numbers are few and DRE assistance is available.

5. Modeling the faith is probably something you already do without knowing it.

6. Be yourself. To whom else could that job be given?

Knowing what is expected of you as a catechist and putting those expectations into perspective should permit you to take an optimistic view of the teaching commitment you have made. Taking a fresh look, in Chapter 2, at the skills you'll bring to this commitment will only add to your growing sense of confidence as an emerging catechist.

How to know if you're ready to teach

Like most catechists, you're a conscientious person who sees religious education as serious business. Before stepping into the classroom, you want to feel confident that you are adequately prepared and fully qualified to teach the faith to children.

Of course, that kind of dedicated approach requires that you measure yourself and your abilities against a reliable and relevant list of qualifications.

You might jump to the conclusion that becoming a volunteer catechist requires you to own a resume that includes:

- A college degree

- Teaching experience

- Coaching or youth leadership positions

- Arts and crafts know-how

- Participation in other church ministries

There is no doubt that such a formidable list contains elements valuable to any volunteer teacher. But it's not the *only* list imaginable.

There is a second possibility, an equally valid list of qualifications that is directly linked to the kinds of tasks that you, as a catechist, will be asked to complete.

Yes, your work may take you into a traditional classroom setting with desks and perhaps even a blackboard, but what you teach will be far removed from a typical school curriculum. Yours is a very different kind of teaching assignment. As a catechist, your job is to share with children a weekly conversation that centers on God.

Volunteers taking on this very special kind of "teaching" can consider themselves well prepared if their background features the collection of abilities and traits reviewed below.

CONVERSATION SKILLS

As a catechist you will be entrusted with passing on some very important information. Your catechist's guide will suggest approaches and teaching tools that will help you to deliver each lesson's message. Still, the solid use of those tools and the meaningful presentation of each message will hinge on your ability to hold a conversation with children.

So consider your experience in talking with, not at, children. If you are a parent, conversation with children is an ongoing part of your life. If you have nieces and nephews or friends with children, you find lots of opportunities to talk with young people. Maybe you employ teens, wait on young people, or have neighbors with children. Possibly you watch television shows in which children play prominent roles.

Certainly you can think of some wonderful conversations you have had with kids. Recall the most enjoyable chats and amusing exchanges, and the things you have learned in dialogue with children. Consider their wonderful curiosity, their ability to question and probe, their dogged search for "why" things are as they are. Can those pleasant, everyday experiences somehow affect your readiness to teach religion to children?

Decidedly, yes. At its best, religious education is about experiencing the faith together. It's a task that begs for more conversation and less oration.

Your informal mini gab-fests with young people have likely convinced you of some important truths. Most notable: children love to talk. They actually want to take part in classroom discussion. They like to contribute. And they can be exceptionally good at it, but they need to be primed, directed, monitored, encouraged, and praised in the process.

That's where your conversational skills come to the fore. During a lifetime filled with discussions you've learned the importance of listening, of not having to control every aspect of a conversation. You are open to questions and willing to lead—but not necessarily dominate—the hunt for solutions. Along the way, you have gathered up quite a repertoire of simple stories, analogies, and examples from daily living that can add a dash of reality and a personal touch to any lesson. It is exactly these skills that will allow you to foster a positive classroom atmosphere in which you and your students can experience a joint effort to grow in knowledge and love of God.

LEARNING EXPERIENCES

Think for a moment about the best teacher you ever had. What clever approaches did he use to encourage an active response from you? What motivational device did she dance out to coax the class to listen and learn? Do you remember what made that teacher so special? Of course you do.

Throughout your school days, each time you went to class,

showed up for soccer practice, or rehearsed with the school band, you had a ringside seat from which to observe how teaching and learning take place. You know lots about teaching; you just learned about it from the student's side of the desk.

Being on the receiving end of education, you had plenty of opportunities to discover what strategies helped you to learn and to notice that other kids didn't always learn in the same way. You became painfully aware of which teaching techniques got your attention and which ones bored you silly. Before you got to high school you could identify what distinguished the really "good" teachers from the not so productive ones.

At home, as a child with siblings, cousins, and friends, or as a parent with children of your own, you learned, sometimes the hard way, the tactics and the value of cooperation. If you put together a lemonade stand with your brothers, organized neighborhood kids to play ball, or kept a young family headed in the right direction, you were simultaneously learning the art of working with children.

It really is possible to pack up those simple lessons learned and take them with you into the more structured setting of the religious education classroom. There you will find that your past has given you solid grounding in what textbooks term "classroom management."

You know how to gently but effectively shut down the boisterous and promote the timid. You've learned, perhaps the hard way, the importance of working within a time frame. You understand what it means to stay on target without losing important details. And you've experienced what it means to inspire people with the strength of your own enthusiasm.

Unintentionally you have gathered up precisely the kind of knowledge that will come to your rescue when you stand before a dozen fifth graders all clamoring to be recognized at once or a collection of second graders who appear to have gone mute.

You won't have all the answers. Who does? But you'll be surprised at how well your practical learning experiences have prepared you for the teaching job ahead.

HOBBIES AND INTERESTS

Religious education classes are made up of more than time filled with reading, writing, and answering questions. The important messages each lesson contains are offered to children through a variety of action-centered teaching techniques.

Arts and crafts are commonly and successfully employed as implements for instruction. But DREs will agree that there is room in religious education for more than just the fun provided by scissors, colored paper, and glitter glue. Music, cooking, acting, gardening, photography, collecting, computers, film, and just about any other individual skill or imaginable pastime can become a fascinating and surprising vehicle for broadening student knowledge of God.

When you become a volunteer catechist, you can't help but bring along your unique gifts and abilities. Just a quick look at your treasury of God-given talents reveals that not only do you have your fair share of gifts, but some of them are ideally suited for use in the classroom.

Those days spent on the stage crew of your school drama club may have left you with some wonderful instincts about how to work an occasional skit into a lesson plan. Your stint in your own garage band may suggest that you bring music into the classroom. And don't forget the hundreds of hours you have logged viewing movies old and new. How many scenes have you watched that provide the perfect spiritual or moral illustration to bring a lesson to life for young people?

Perhaps you aren't a former opera star or whiz on the computer, but each gift you do possess has the potential to become a bridge that connects you to your students. Maximizing the use of your particular gifts will provide you with exciting, student-friendly opportunities to bring God into the lives of children.

FAITH

For many catechists, the nitty-gritty of sharing the faith with children is a very challenging proposition. Lessons can quickly revolve into situations in which you are asked to open up a bit and talk with children about something you may rarely articulate at all—your faith. Until this point in your life you likely have considered your faith a rather private matter, something you and God are still working on together.

How can you be asked to guide children along a path that you are still trying to negotiate? What if they sense that you have your own questions, doubts, and concerns? What if they guess correctly that you are still learning and growing too?

Everyone knows how easily kids can see through pretense. They pick up on anything that hints of insincerity. Any word spoken that is fake or false will not get by even the youngest child.

Ironically, it is this insightfulness of children that will actually make your job a little easier than anticipated. They may well recognize your uncertainties. At the same time they won't miss for a moment that you bring with you the great equalizer, the ultimate qualification for any catechist. They'll sense early on that, even though you struggle with it, your faith is important to you.

Just take an honest look at your own faith life. Put aside the bumps along the road and the turns better left untaken.

Instead, examine closely the powerful effect of faith-laden friendships, Christian examples informally set before you, bits of Scripture heard and held, compassionate deeds done and received, moments of immense natural beauty that have stirred you and still do.

Somewhere in the midst of all those experiences and encounters, your faith has slowly emerged and become central to who you are. Even now your faith is nudging you along to serve as a catechist.

That same faith is ready to bolster your teaching efforts with enthusiasm, sincerity, and humility.

When you step into the classroom you won't have all your faith issues resolved. But what you will have is exactly what children will mark and respect: a willingness to continue your own important journey of faith in the company of children.

QUALIFIED?

So now perhaps you can smile to yourself when occasionally someone suggests that you are a very nice person, but just not someone with "the stuff" to be a catechist.

You know better. It turns out you have been preparing for this kind of volunteer work all your life. You aren't starting off unprepared. You know how to talk with children. You have experienced on your own how learning happens. You are the owner of a unique assortment of skills and hobbies that can enhance almost any lesson. You have grown in faith by moving about in a world full of caring, loving people and magnificent natural wonders. The faith is so important to you that you are ready to share it with others.

Oh, you're the real deal all right. You've got exactly "the stuff" of which catechists are made.

 ## Questions

Share with others or reflect by yourself on each of the following.

What difference would it make and to whom if you decided not to serve as a catechist?

During your student days, what one thing did you observe about teaching or teachers that might improve your teaching performance?

What two skills, unrelated to arts and crafts, are you prepared to use to develop a lesson?

What favorite bit of Scripture do you most easily associate with your work as a catechist?

What family experiences taught you the most about working with children?

How to teach well for sixty minutes

Experience confirms that sixty minutes—the average length of a class meeting—can truly fly by when you spend that time watching an action movie, lounging on the beach, or shopping with friends. The same sixty minutes can drag on endlessly when you find yourself in front of a dozen or more children who want to be instructed and entertained at the same time.

What can you do to make sure that the first class hour you teach and all those that follow pass productively and enjoyably for you and your students?

Don't look for a magic formula or a complex solution; what works best is sticking to the basics. Know where you are going and how you are going to get there. Stay on topic and on time. Don't forget to include a personal touch. These simple guidelines will see you through from minute one to minute sixty of any classroom hour.

SO WHERE ARE YOU GOING? (MESSAGE)
Whether you are going out by yourself or with friends, for

a half hour or a few weeks, you seldom leave home without knowing your destination.

Why not apply that same commonsense awareness when you set out to share a lesson with a group of children? In fact, don't ask students to open a book or turn a page unless you know in advance in what direction the day's lesson is headed and what message it is meant to share.

Each week, before you meet with students, discover this key direction information by turning to the catechist's guide and carefully reading through the lesson plan for the upcoming class.

When you finish your review, organize your thoughts by writing a single sentence that summarizes the lesson's message. Create that sentence by asking yourself what one idea the author wants students to remember. What essential point do you hope children will take home from class? What central concept do you want them to be able to recall when they return next week?

Message summaries look and sound like these sample sentences.

- *For a Lesson on Prayer:* "Prayer is one way of opening ourselves to God's waiting love."

- *For a Lesson on Love:* "Jesus teaches us to value and care for one another as God the Father values and cares for us."

- *For a Lesson on Service*: "We are called to live God's law of love by serving the needs of others."

By assembling your summary sentence, you have completed the first step toward teaching well for sixty minutes. You have established the message of the lesson clearly in your mind.

You know where you are going.

Stay on message

Message summary sentences are remarkable because they both define and confine. While clearly expressing where you are going, the message summary simultaneously sets the borders within which you should teach during the class hour.

Of course, once you begin normal classroom exchanges, you should expect to find yourself in situations that tempt you to wander outside of those suggested borders. You reason to yourself...

> "I don't really feel comfortable teaching this lesson. I think I'll substitute a topic I know more about."

> "I wish I had taken the time to prepare this lesson. Maybe I'll just expand on what we did last week."

> "The kids are starting to drift. They'll tune in more if I talk about stuff they like."

The truth is you will find yourself less confident about teaching some lessons than others. There will be weeks when you get caught short of preparation time. And some teaching messages will immediately click with students while others will seem to fall flat.

When you arrive at such crossroads, and we all do, you may feel a strong urge to go off topic. That's exactly the time to remember that, as a catechist, you are responsible for respecting both the work of the trained professionals who wrote the texts and the authority of the bishops who approved them.

Much thought and planning has gone into producing text

lessons that match the learning abilities and content needs of children. The topics you teach have been arranged in a logical sequence, each building on what was learned in the previous lesson while laying the foundation for what is to follow. Once you step away from the planned message, you interrupt the flow of learning, run the risk of totally missing key elements, and handicap both you and your students when you attempt to move on to the next lesson.

To make the best use of the sixty minutes you share with students, avoid the call to wander, skip over the desire to freelance, and concentrate on delivering the message.

HOW TO GET WHERE YOU'RE GOING (MANAGEMENT)

Knowing where you are going and then staying on message represent only part of your teaching assignment. You also need to know how to get where you are going, and that means deciding how to manage the lesson.

What will you and the students say and do between the opening prayer and the closing blessing that will move the lesson's message off the page and into their hearts and minds? There is no one simple answer. In fact, the path you take to manage a lesson's message and get you where you want to go will likely change from week to week.

Depending on the nature of each lesson's message, the catechist's guide will present you with a distinct set of teaching options like games, puzzles, movies, small-group activities, crafts, reading, or full-class discussions. The DRE may offer additional resource suggestions or directions about which lesson management devices are best suited to you and your particular teaching situation. Often the final selection of teaching tools will be left to you.

When you have made your choices, recall how you assembled the message summary sentence, and in the same way condense the management plan into an abbreviated list that describes how you will proceed in sharing the message.

For example, perhaps you have decided to begin a lesson with an opening prayer that immediately focuses students on the lesson's message. Next you plan to move on with a suggested reading from the student text that begins to develop that message. To further engage children, you choose to invite them to participate in small-group skits framed by the catechist's guide. A reasonable follow-up could be a full-class discussion of the skits just offered. The final reflection—reenforcing the message and asking for God's guidance in living out that message—might then conclude the hour.

With those teaching steps in mind, your management summary list might be: "Prayer, reading, skits, group discussion, reflection."

Armed with a management summary, you will no longer be working from a ten-page lesson that, at a glance, appears to be filled with dozens of unrelated paragraphs. You now own a descriptive outline that reminds you how the lesson is divided and in what order you plan to present it. You have figured out how to manage the lesson. You know how to get where you're going.

Stay on time

Your management summary does more than just effectively order your classroom activities. It suggests the need to divide the available sixty minutes among the several activities you plan to complete.

Your guide may furnish you with specific directions about the number of minutes you should spend on each part of the lesson development. A few general thoughts about time usage are also worth your attention.

- An unstructured opening prayer or lesson introduction can gobble up precious time without adding much to the lesson. It is possible to blend the two elements by first introducing the lesson briefly and then offering an opening prayer that invites God's guidance as you work through the lesson. Connecting the two can save you minutes that can be better spent elsewhere in the lesson.

- As you divide the class hour in your mind, save the largest chunk of time for what you determine to be the central activity of the lesson.

- Limit the number of labor-intensive, time-devouring activities in any lesson to one.

- Encourage students' topic-centered questions, but rein in distractions.

- Stop five-to-ten minutes before the end of the class hour and share a concise lesson review that enables children to take the lesson's message home with them.

- Recognize the distinct possibility that you could run out of lesson before you run out of time. Always plan beyond your plan. Prepare a backup scheme in which you invite children to look ahead to next week's lesson or connect the current lesson to their daily living.

With these suggestions in mind, consider how you might organize one hour of class time to manage the lesson summarized above as: "Prayer, reading, skits, group discussion, reflection."

How much time would you allot to each of the elements in that lesson?

One possible arrangement might be:

OPENING PRAYER . . . . 5 MINUTES
READING . . . . 10 MINUTES
SKITS . . . . 30 MINUTES
GROUP DISCUSSION . . . . 10 MINUTES
CLOSING REFLECTION . . . . 5 MINUTES

In this time scheme, the "opening prayer" and "closing reflection" are intentionally limited to five minutes. Because they are framing activities, "reading" and "group discussion" are given more time than the opening and closing, but a good deal less time than the main focus of the lesson. By dividing sixty minutes in this way, you effectively carve out a full half-hour of class time in which to concentrate on preparation and performance of skits, your central teaching activity.

Keep in mind that there are many ways to organize and present the same teaching message. By combining specific directions from your guide and these general suggestions with your own understanding of your students' talents and limitations, you can produce a lesson that neatly fits the allotted time and delivers the lesson's message.

INCLUDING A PERSONAL TOUCH

Putting together a solid sixty-minute lesson rests chiefly on discovering the lesson's message and lining up techniques to deliver it. But teaching "well" demands one additional step. The well-taught lesson requires you to breathe life into the lesson by drawing out and relying on the human elements present—you and your students.

With a little investigation you'll uncover a surprising number of openings that encourage you and your students to step up and put your personal stamp on almost any lesson. You can begin to enrich lessons by including catechist and student experiences, encounters, and interests while staying within the message boundaries and the management time frame. Just make sure to limit references to those that fulfill the following teaching needs.

Clarifying
Even in the best-written texts, you will encounter instances in which the vocabulary used or the context in which ideas are presented is not a perfect match for the level of student comprehension. Because clarity is absent, the meaning of particular words, sentences, or paragraphs, or the general thrust of the lesson, may be lost on some children. In these instances, by drawing on your own experiences or those of students, you can provide the kind of substance and understanding that will translate unfamiliar terms or concepts and draw children back into a lesson.

Humanizing
Even well-understood ideas can become more meaningful when fleshed out by the addition of a personal, human dimension. For example, students may read in the text that "Getting to church on Sunday can be difficult." While students understand the meaning of the sentence, you and your class have the ability to flavor that concept, to make it more interesting and even memorable.

By sharing your own personal experiences of dashing off to church at the last moment, you add an element of interest and also prompt students to share their own encounters with this simple truth. In the process, you bring the words on the page to life and allow children to see themselves as truly connected to the reading. "Getting to church on Sunday can be difficult" is no longer just a textbook item. It becomes a shared experience between you and the class.

Localizing

Religious education textbooks are created for use across the entire country. While the truths they contain are the same for us all, the students' ability to recognize and apply those truths in their own particular living circumstances may not always be addressed by the general language used in the text.

The simple input of catechists and classmates can help children to see the full meaning of words and ideas in their own daily lives. "Prayer," "service," and "sin" are words children can understand in a general sense, but these words can have far greater meaning if they are presented to them in the context of their everyday experiences and environment.

By appropriately referencing your own experiences and encounters and inviting your students to share theirs, you can clarify, humanize, and localize the message of your lesson and share joint ownership of the learning experience.

Very little happens by chance in the classroom. Teaching for sixty minutes will end up feeling as long or as short as you plan to make it.

Questions

Share with others or reflect by yourself on each of the following.

If you were unsure of the message of this week's lesson, how might that negatively affect your teaching?

With what types of development techniques are you most comfortable: reading, small group, crafts, individual sharing, other? Why?

Can you share an example of a teaching experience in which you wandered way off the lesson's message? Do you remember why that happened?

Do you remember the last time you finished the assigned lesson well ahead of the class hour? How did you fill the remaining minutes?

What is the class's reaction when you add personal comments to help make a point? After those comments, do you find it difficult to get back on track?

How to motivate students

By itself, a well-constructed lesson that shares a meaningful message should hold the attention of most students. What stands in the way of that kind of anticipated, positive result is often just human nature.

Children are naturally inquisitive, self-involved, and action-oriented. Those characteristics frequently act to block students' concentration, making it difficult for catechists to break through and engage them in the lesson.

By inserting strategies that add focus, connection, and action to your lesson plan, you can successfully turn would-be obstructions into tools to fire up and sustain student interest throughout the class hour.

FOCUS

Have you ever gathered students around a table and put down a map to let them follow the flight of the Holy Family or the missionary travels of St. Paul? Ever worn a T-shirt to colorfully announce an upcoming service event your class is planning to attend? What about calling class to order in a prayer corner that features an open Bible and a candle? If these kinds of activities sound familiar, then it's likely you already have a head start on using a focus with your students.

For teaching purposes, a focus can be any item—large or small, one or multidimensional, solid or liquid—that has the capacity to grab and hold student attention.

A word written in large letters on a chalkboard, a First Communion photo, a pitcher of water—all these items and many more have the potential to be focal points for a lesson. What makes them more than just random items of passing interest is the fact that each can also furnish added meaning and depth to a particular teaching theme.

For example, if your class was about to begin to study the sacraments, your focus could be the word "SIGN" written boldly on the board. Starting with this single word, you could then move on to construct a simple definition of the word "sacrament."

Leaving the word "SIGN" on the board throughout the class would continually remind students that sacraments are in fact signs of God's continuing love and care for us.

Of course, you might also choose to open the same lesson using a First Communion picture as a focus, as this would provide an easily understood image of what one particular sacrament looks like. In the same way, a pitcher of water could remind students of the first sacrament, baptism.

These three items are but a few examples of the focus items you might select to open a discussion about sacraments. None is hard to come by; all act as direct links to the lesson topic. Each succeeds in centering students and expanding their understanding of the lesson's message.

While frequently used to call students into a lesson at the very beginning of class, focus items can be used with similar effect at other junctures of lesson development. Producing a focus to set the tone for a mid-class craft project, a peer conversation, or a text reading can serve to reestablish a lesson's message or shade its meaning.

In your first few attempts at using a focus, especially with younger children, try out common items that seem to tie in to the lesson directly but also give it a slightly new look. A lesson that features the apostle Peter might benefit from the presence of a sizeable rock set on a centrally located table. Examining that rock together—its rough and smooth edges, its firmness, its ability to roll along—can help children to understand the very human qualities that made Peter, "the rock," a perfect choice to lead Christ's church on earth.

Older children may be more drawn in by a focus that has a less obvious, more mysterious link to the lesson. Something as basic as an empty paper sack can be used to help children focus on the emptiness felt by the apostles in the time between the death and resurrection of Jesus; so too could a flashlight with no battery. Your choice of focus items rests, in the end, on your vision and the comprehension skills of your students.

It won't take long for you to incorporate the focus into your weekly lesson plans because it plays to the natural inquisitiveness of children. By stirring their imagination, lifting children up and out of the ordinary, and prompting novel and unexpected lines of discussion, a well-chosen focus can enhance interest in any lesson.

CONNECTION

Everyone likes to feel that any subject being discussed is at least in part about them. People like to imagine themselves filling a key role in a movie or taking up the goals of the main character in a book. Children especially like to be positioned

center stage in almost anything that is happening.
From a teaching perspective, that means the sooner you
help students to locate themselves in the lesson, the sooner
they will respond enthusiastically and begin to take part.
By thoughtfully referencing their interests, concerns, and
day-to-day living as the background against which faith-sharing takes place, you can make children both the subject and
interested participants of every lesson you teach.

As you move through any lesson, you will find that common
lesson elements like introduction, prayer, development, and
review provide clear avenues to encourage learning by linking
students with content. At each juncture you can reassert your
efforts to make students feel a part of what is happening in the
classroom and thereby motivate them to get and stay involved.

Introduction

It doesn't matter whether it's a television show, a phone conversation, or a movie; usually we know in the first few minutes
whether or not we are going to be motivated to continue to
pay attention. Children react quickly and in the same way to
how you introduce the week's lesson.

Making an attempt to connect with children at the very outset of class is well worth the little extra planning it requires.
The way you offer a chapter to your students sets the tone for
everything that follows. There is no doubt that it is much easier to awaken student interest at the very beginning of a class
than to try to reengage them once they have shut down.

You'll find hints about how to connect with your students by
looking at the weekly chapter title or subtitles. As you're framing your introduction, try to put yourself in the place of your
students. Hear your opening sentence as they would hear it.

If today's lesson is about the sacraments, which introductory sentence do you think would be more appealing to them?

A. "Today we are going to study about the sacraments."
Or B. "How many sacraments have you already received?"

If you said "B" you are probably correct. Sentence B is more likely to motivate students to continue listening because it seems to say: "This lesson is going to be about you, and I need your help to develop it."

Other introductory sentences might be:

- "Have you ever been to a baptism?"

- "What do you remember most about your First Communion?"

- "Do you think confirmation will make a difference in you?"

Each of these introductory sentences attempts to engage students immediately by replacing a general lesson theme with something more personal and therefore more interesting. They are not difficult to construct; they just require teacher awareness of the need to connect.

Prayer

By its very essence prayer is a method for connection. In fact, opening or closing prayers are less about reading or reciting the right words and more about the connection the chosen words can achieve between those who are praying and God.

By welcoming students into the process of prayer, you encourage them to be central actors in its creation and offering. With younger children, this may mean helping them to add their own heartfelt petitions to a class prayer. Older students can feel at the center when asked to provide or lead a prayer by and for the group.

By teaching children to craft prayer that includes their thoughts, concerns, and needs, and requires their participation, you motivate them to come off the sidelines and connect directly to what is happening in their classroom.

Lesson development

Children will stay motivated as you develop the lesson if you lead them to broaden the topic and position themselves in its midst. Forming connections as you develop a lesson means remembering that the lesson can't just be about prayer, the commandments, the Mass, or an element of church history. The lesson must also be about a student's involvement with and connection to those themes.

Open their eyes to this connection by encouraging student participation to help shape the lesson as it moves forward. Each time a student participates by answering a question, giving an example, expanding a plan, or personalizing a concept, together you will notice that the lesson is improved and made more original.

Giving children a sense of their ownership of a lesson through connection motivates them to be attentive. What they add to the lesson as it proceeds will make the lesson unique and memorable.

Review

Even the final lesson review can open the door to student connection. Don't be limited only to standard summary questions. Be on the lookout for ways in which students can utilize their own skill set to illustrate, act out, or retell a composite version of the day's lesson.

Making a solid connection doesn't require altering your basic teaching plan. Motivating students doesn't mean straying from the model of knowing where you're going and how you're going to get there. What is necessary is for you to take advantage of those instances within that framework that allow the lesson not just to be *for* the children but also to be *about* the children.

ACTION

You don't have to be with children in a classroom for more than ten minutes to recognize how much they like to move. Sitting still even for short periods of time is not something they do by choice.

As a catechist you have two alternatives. You can apply all your energy to limiting the turning, reaching, twisting, shuffling, and leaning that find their way into the classroom. A simpler suggestion is to find ways to redirect their actions, turning them into learning tools instead of classroom distractions.

Positively tapping into children's shared desire to move requires you to keep in mind these guidelines:

■ Recognize motion as an aid for your existing lesson plan, not a substitute. Motion should be used to bring children enthusiastically into the previously planned lesson to achieve particular results. Don't have children move just for the sake of motion.

■ For each lesson, arrange at least three instances that require children to participate in some kind of action.

■ Use as wide a variety of students' motion options as possible, including:
   » *Changing seating arrangements to work in pairs, small groups, or circle*

34

» *Standing up to give a response*
» *Raising hands to express a vote*
» *Passing out work, equipment, tools*
» *Moving for crafts, review games, learning relays*
» *Standing to view a map or other focus*
» *Changing position for prayer or film*

■ Remember to include motion in your own teaching style.
  » *Don't remain sitting or standing throughout a class. Alternate your position and your location in the classroom.*
  » *Move to share a focus, emphasize a point, check on student work, or make your presence known.*
  » *Animate your lesson with dramatic gestures when appropriate.*
  » *Move to pass out or collect work.*

Regardless of the age group you teach, most children will present themselves as people who have inquiring minds, who center on themselves, and who are action oriented. Your job is not necessarily to train them out of these habits. Instead, as a volunteer teacher, you can learn to take advantage of these natural tendencies and use them to motivate your students and drive your lesson.

 *Questions*

Share with others or reflect by yourself on each of the following.

Who is more difficult for you to teach, a child who is overly inquisitive, or completely self-involved, or highly rambunctious? Explain your choice.

What success or difficulties have you had with using focus items in the past? How do you account for why the focus worked or didn't work?

What elements of daily living provide points of connection for catechists when teaching children?

What is your normal position when teaching? In what ways and how often do you attempt to change that posture?

How to use small-group activities

Some experienced catechists use the small-group activity teaching technique as often as possible; others use it with less frequency. That minor difference aside, most would willingly agree that knowing *how* to use small-group activities in the classroom effectively adds a major teaching tool to any catechist's collection.

Even if you are comfortable with how you currently prepare and present lessons for a traditional classroom setting, you really shouldn't pass on the chance to investigate the value of teaching via the small-group activity.

WHAT SMALL-GROUP ACTIVITIES LOOK LIKE

When your DRE or catechist's guide directs you to use a small-group activity to develop a lesson, they are usually asking you to take two simple steps. First, move students from their customary seating arrangement into groups of three to six students meeting around a common table. Second, advise students that their work in this new setting is a shared activity that depends for its success on everyone's participation.

The reason for the change in venue will quickly become evident to you and the students. Working in small groups permits children to pursue a wide variety of joint ventures that would be difficult to accomplish in standard-classroom seating. For example, students in small groups have the space they need to take on collective art projects like creating a collage, filling a scrapbook, or completing a mural. Skits or role-play exercises that require room for active participation also find a comfortable fit in small-group settings.

Clustering children produces a cooperative atmosphere perfect for reviewing a movie, preparing a group prayer, planning a class service project, pooling lenten or Advent ideas, writing group letters, responding to topical questions, or brainstorming on suggested themes.

Moving students from a full-class to a small-group setting doesn't change the lesson topic; it changes the lesson format. Small groups will look different, sound different, and feel different from a full class, but the learning activities performed in the group will address the same lesson message. Repeated experiences with this new format will allow you and your students to gradually feel at home and benefit from working in this arrangement.

HOW TO PREPARE FOR A SMALL-GROUP ACTIVITY

Deciding to use a small-group activity will require some changes in your regular lesson preparation. You will still need to read through the lesson, and it still will be important to have a clear understanding of the lesson's message. Beyond that, small-group activities charge you with the added responsibility of equipping groups to share the core of the lesson among themselves and, for the most part, separated from you and the rest of the class.

You job is to funnel the lesson's message through small groups using the medium of a shared-learning experience. Taking the following steps will help you to prepare for lessons that find their core in a small-group activity.

Review the lesson and the group activity
Begin preparation to teach a lesson using small groups just as you would prepare for any other lesson. Read the chapter material thoroughly and uncover the lesson's message. Reduce the message—in your mind or on a piece of paper—to one or two summary sentences.

Make certain that you fully understand the group activity suggested by the catechist's guide or the DRE, and how that activity will allow students to explore the lesson's message.

Once you have a solid comprehension of the lesson's message, the basics of the suggested group activity, and how the two are connected, you are ready to translate what you know into language students can readily understand.

Create an Instruction Sheet
Students can be expected to take on a group activity only when they have a clear understanding of the lesson's goal and how the activity will lead them to achieve it. A well-formed instruction sheet can accomplish those ends.

Each group should receive enough instruction sheets for all members. According to the activity and student needs, instructions might include some or all of the following:

- A clear statement of the lesson's message, the group activity, and the connection between the two

- A concise, specific list of ordered steps the group should take to carry out the learning activity

- Individual tasks each student must complete within the group setting

- A statement of the end product expected as a result of the group activity (e.g., skit, a summary statement, drawings, answers to questions)

- A timetable for completion of the activity

It is important, especially when working with younger children, to review the instruction sheet aloud with the entire class before dividing into groups. Offering the directions in a full-class setting reduces the number of times you will need to clarify directions or answer common questions.

Reorganize the class into groups
Knowing the nature of the planned group activity, you can determine how to divide the class into workable units.

The activity itself will often dictate the optimum number of students in the group. A rule of thumb would suggest not less than three (unless it is obviously a pairs activity) and no more than six (larger groups create excessive noise and can be unwieldy).

Determining the precise makeup of each group is sometimes more problematic. It may seem natural to let students form their own groups, but that approach can leave more reserved students on the sidelines or collect too many like-minded students around a table.

While catechist-created groups are preferable, they will require time and thought. Good judgment, sensitivity, and practice will help you to put together combinations of students who can work together and treat each other respectfully in the process.

Reformat the room

Given the activity and group size you have planned, consider the available space and furniture; then rearrange both to accommodate your teaching plan. Space the groups in a way that allows for separate conversations and movement and minimizes mutual interference or interruption.

Plan when and how to carry out the necessary room changes with the least disruption and in the shortest amount of time. Make certain that your lesson plan includes time to reset the room, leaving it as you found it.

With advice from the DRE, consider how to reduce any negative effects the planned activity might have on adjoining classes. And, of course, inform neighboring catechists in advance about the likelihood of slightly elevated noise levels.

Collect and prepare necessary supplies or equipment

It is frightening how quickly group work can founder on the absence of what seem to be insignificant supplies. To avoid near disasters, mentally tick through the steps of the activity and list what materials are required along the way.

Carefully count out supplies and then make sure you have extra copies of scissors, props, instruction sheets, and whatever you are using or can imagine you might need. Don't leave anything to chance.

Finally, pack all materials in the order that will allow you easy access and distribution.

THE RESULTS OF SMALL-GROUP ACTIVITIES

As the comprehensive list above suggests, small-group activities do require more and different preparation than what is normally needed. As the activity unfolds, so will the multifaceted returns on your investment of time and energy.

Perhaps most noticeable, when a small-group activity is used, your active teaching role is minimized. Once you set the project into motion, your participation is as limited as you choose to make it. Without much additional involvement on your part, small-group projects automatically generate motivational elements like focus, connection, and action that together prime the pump for productive learning experiences.

Focus

By their nature, most group activities will require equipment or supplies. You distribute project material like a map, a sample craft, a blank poster board, or a bag of costumes to each group. But what you are also doing is handing each group a ready-made focus item that at once grabs student attention and begins to direct their thoughts and actions.

Connection

Because they summon the participation of all, small-group projects can shift the pressure from the individual child to the group, creating a more relaxed learning environment for all. As each student gradually takes on his or her particular part of the group work, they feel a personal responsibility for, attachment to, and pride in the overall group result. Activities done together allow each group member to connect in their own individual way to the lesson's message.

Action

Small-group activities require children to get up and move from their standard seated position and re-form into collective arrangements. This means that before a paper is passed or a book is consulted, students are involved in motion that is pumping energy into whatever lesson message is about to be opened.

As the group sets to work, you will notice that each activity contains its own unique motion requirements. Children have little choice but to abandon classroom postures like sitting and looking straight ahead at you or at a book and replace them by freely turning, leaning, talking, pointing, cutting, gluing, gesturing, acting, and feeling more like themselves.

Fringe benefits
With the activity in full swing, you will have the opportunity to observe some of the more subtle rewards that spring from small-group work.

■ Small-group activities have the capacity to turn students into capable teaching assistants. Drawing on their own energy, not yours, students confront the activity. With just an instruction sheet to guide them, they probe, analyze, evaluate, express, and even consider how to apply the lesson's message to daily living.

■ Because each group is a unique combination of children, each group provides its own special avenue for lesson enrichment. Group work provides a comfort zone where reluctant students become more willing to get involved; it opens the classroom to the sound of new voices seldom heard in the ordinary class setting. These voices bring novel viewpoints and texture to the lesson. Thoughts formerly left unexpressed find their way to the surface, thanks to the informality of the small-group experience.

■ Not only do small groups provide students with new learning options; they provide both you and your students the chance to see each other from unusual perspectives. When groups are fully occupied with the activity at hand, you are free to visit with individual members and take note of who they are and what gifts they own. As you wander among the students, they also have a chance to become aware of you as an interesting and caring individual.

- Hiding in each small-group activity are endless and unpredictable opportunities for interpersonal encounters among students that teach cooperation, sharing, understanding, and appreciation for the skills and individuality of others. These chances for Christian growth appear to occur with greater frequency in small groups than in the more isolated configuration of a standard classroom.

- In those instances when your normal classroom routine is starting to feel old and worn out, small-group activities have the power to reinvigorate catechists and students. The changes in seating, learning style, and required skills provide growth for the entire class that lasts even into the next class meeting.

ORGANIZATIONAL REMINDERS

When you finally come face to face with the prospect of using a small-group activity as a teaching tool, these organization reminders may prove useful.

- Start small. Your first small-group activity should have a limited objective, brief directions, and few moving parts. Expand next time as your results indicate.

- Review your small-group activity with your DRE in advance. She may have specific hints or tips about the space or materials you plan to use.

- Carefully monitor the progress of activities, applying the brake or the gas as needed to finish within the allotted time. Have related backup work on hand for early finishers.

- Accept as fact that moving students into groups will cause some noise and disruption. But insist that groups progressively learn how to manage an orderly transfer from one format to another.

- Use small-group activities only when they can make an authentic contribution to sharing the faith.

- Recognize that completely backing away from small-group activities surrenders opportunities for productive experiences that cannot always be duplicated in traditional seating arrangements.

 *Questions*

Share with others or reflect by yourself on each of the following.

Before you read this chapter what was your general opinion of small-group activities? How did you arrive at this opinion?

Having read the chapter, what still concerns you about the use of small groups?

What do you see as the most important reason to give small groups a try?

Considering the personalities and chemistry of the class you currently teach, how would you expect them to respond to the introduction of a small-group activity? Will their response make it easier or more difficult to offer small-group activities?

Teaching
with the arts

Catechists and students agree: approaching the subject of God is one mind-boggling assignment. Textbooks help, but restricting teaching and learning efforts to just reading the words of the text would deny everyone the chance to explore God in all God's wonder.

Fortunately, DREs and catechist guides acknowledge the need for catechists and students to step away from the textbook from time to time and develop the lesson's message by alternate means. With unreserved enthusiasm and frequency, they suggest you consider teaching with the arts.

WHY WELCOME THE ARTS IN THE CLASSROOM?
For any well-prepared teacher, not just the artists among us, using the arts as a teaching tool should present no unusual complications. Broadening your understanding of what the arts include and how they function in the classroom will likely increase your willingness to welcome the arts as a reliable teaching tool.

More than just crayons and glue

The "arts" cover a large and ever-expanding list of creative activities like painting, music, dance, drama, photography, and handcrafts. Such major art forms readily subdivide into other related creative formats. For example, drama can include mime, role-play, skits, dialog, pageants, reenactments, and film. Handcrafts might be pursued through stenciling, pottery, drawing, or weaving.

In the classroom, each art form presents a novel pathway along which you can lead students to explore and express their understanding of God.

Meant for limited use

Though filled with instructional potential, collectively the arts represent only one of many lesson development plans. Recognizing the arts as a productive teaching option doesn't compel you to prepare an arts-centered adventure to accompany every lesson you teach.

To the contrary, you can serve up arts activities with the best results when you use them in rotation with other comparable teaching aids like puzzles, games, contests, debates, reading, brainstorming, paired discussions, and service projects. Like every other teaching aid, the arts are meant to be applied to those specific situations where they offer a predictably successful fit for you, your class, and the scheduled lesson.

You don't need to be a pro

Using arts as a teaching technique doesn't require you to be even an average artist in any medium. Your inclination to use a particular hymn to make a teaching point doesn't mean you have to be able to sing the tune flawlessly yourself. In fact, it can be your frank and humble display of your own artistic limitations that helps draw out the participation of other reluctant, arts-challenged, self-conscious students.

Instead of modeling the arts, teachers are encouraged to use arts activities to call forth all manner of creative individual student responses from which children can learn more about God and the faith.

The arts give you flexibility
Most art-related projects lend themselves to your particular instructional needs. Art activities can be expanded or simplified according to the dictates of your schedule. The same basic project will often work well whether you assign its completion to groups, pairs, or individuals. Arts projects can be stored and revisited over two or more consecutive weeks or even later in the year when such arrangements suit your purpose and room is available.

Contrary to popular impression, using the arts to develop a lesson need not result in noise, mess, or chaos. Keeping the needs of your students and the lesson in mind, you have leeway to structure art activities to be enjoyable, instructive, and mutually supportive.

The arts help get the job done
What the arts create is more than just fluff, recreation, or something cute to bring home to parents. You can count on the arts, in all their diversity, to help you reveal the message of a lesson in a pleasant and ordered environment.

WHY KIDS RESPOND TO THE ARTS
Announce an arts activity, and you'll hear nearly unanimous student approval. The reasons for this positive reaction can be as many and varied as the children in your classroom.

Arts offer a change

When you offer children the chance to join in an art project, you hold out the promise of change. After a full day or week of school and homework centered on pencil, paper, and books, children respond well to a chance to do something that is totally different and fun.

The arts in any form fill the bill because they allow children alternative ways of learning. They encourage children to move from passive to active and from silent to vocal learners. It doesn't really matter whether the project asks students to work on a mural, join in a skit, or cut pictures for a collage. Children find the sheer variety offered by the arts to be mentally and physically liberating, and so they respond with a smile.

Succeeding by being themselves

The ground rules for success when working with the arts are substantially different from those of other organized learning and playing options. The goal when using the arts to learn about God is not individual achievement or perfection as determined by an arbitrary standard or grading system. Children discover that the key to success in working with the arts is simply to express themselves and how they feel or think about God. The arts remove external judging from the mix and provide a neutral medium in which children can simply relax and express themselves as they develop their own relationship with God.

A chance connection

Offering a variety of arts-centered projects means multiplying the opportunities for children to find a new favorite pathway to explore their experience of God, one that resonates with them in a special way.

For children who struggle with traditional reading and writing exercises, creative art formats supply a totally new means of expression without vocabulary or grammar. This language lets them connect with God in ways that a written text or memorized prayer may not. A simple song, a free-hand sketch, and a grace-filled dance are all avenues of connection to sample and from which to choose.

A change in context
The teachings of the Catholic Church are filled with many heavy, serious themes. Teaching the faith through the arts allows you to gently filter that sometimes somber context while still maintaining the message. You can use beauty and joy, which are so much a part of the arts, to lightly pave over the rough spots and shape smooth edges and soft corners without eroding the teaching.

Inclusion in the conversation
Using the arts gives some students a new sense of involvement in the ongoing classroom discussion of God. The arts provide some students with a "voice" that previously had remained silent. They are and feel themselves to be active, worthwhile, and contributing participants in the journey toward knowing, loving, and serving God. They enjoy the arts because they are experiencing the truth that art empowers.

Heightened accessibility
Teaching children through the arts supplies them with friendly bridges to the mysteries of faith. Being able to sing, dance, act, construct, or produce works that venture toward God makes God more accessible, more part of their experience and their world.

TEACHING A LESSON WITH THE ARTS

No matter how teacher- and student-friendly the arts may be, they are most effective as teaching tools when their use is a structured part of a well-planned lesson. Teaching with the arts does not require a major alteration in your common method of lesson preparation.

The Message

As always, prepare by reading through the text of the lesson. Determine first what the teaching message is and reduce that message, in your mind or on paper, to one or two sentences. Because it is easy for students and teachers to get distracted by the art work itself as it is rolled out, plan to present the lesson's message clearly from the outset.

Imagine, for instance, that the day's lesson is about recognizing God as creator and that your development will involve the planting of seeds and painting of flower pots.

You might open the lesson by saying: "Today we are going to fill flower pots with soil, plant a few seeds, and then paint the pots so that you can take them home to show your family." While it sounds pleasant enough, that kind of introduction skips by the main teaching point of the lesson and focuses on the art work that is, after all, only a tool. Children could easily assume that the planting and decorating functions are really what this lesson is all about.

The same project is more correctly introduced with words like: "Today's lesson is about God's creative power, the beauty God has created, and how we can act as God's helpers in caring for that beauty. Let's take a look at what we can do to serve God's plan with these simple seeds and soil." In this way you have made the point that the lesson is not about who can create the most beautiful pot; it's about doing our part to care for the beautiful world that God has created using the tools God has provided.

Begin each arts-enhanced lesson by connecting students to the faith message to be shared. Then, in a secondary way, you can move on to explain the steps by which the message will be developed through a non-competitive use of the arts.

Encourage participation from all students regardless of art talent. Remind students as work goes on that the lesson is not about who can be the best artist, designer, dancer, or musician. It is about displaying the beauty of God's creation through tools God has given us. That's a message everyone can get on board with.

The Management

Your review of the text lesson will help you to picture the suggested art-centered teaching tool and the way it is to be used in the classroom. In a few sentences, summarize that project and the steps necessary to achieve it. Share this information with students in age-appropriate terms.

List the project steps in abbreviated form on the board or on half sheets that you can distribute to each student. Continuing with the flower pot example from above, the steps might be as simple as:

■ Decorate the pot with paints or stickers

■ Fill the pot with prepared soil

■ With your finger press a small hole into soil

■ Put a few seeds into the hole

■ Water gently

You need not be concerned about motivating students to join in most art projects. Quite routinely, arts-centered activities contain those three familiar motivational devices: focus, connection, and action.

Focus Whether students are working individually or in small groups, they will find a focus in the very materials that are to be used. Such material as colored paper, skit costumes, a film, or completed project samples all grab student attention and invite them to get involved in the activity at hand. No need to plan an additional focus—the arts have provided one for you.

Connection Students seldom disconnect themselves from arts projects. With little hesitation, most students hear and respond to the call from the arts to put themselves—with their feelings, views, and ideas—in the spotlight. The likelihood that this lesson is going to have a lot to do with what is important to them is a powerful draw for even easily distracted students.

Action Students react positively to the call issued by most arts projects to stand, walk, reach, pass, dance, form groups, or move in unison. Almost every student arts activity is likely not just to suggest but to actually require a range of motion not found in the ordinary text lesson. Action is the passion of children. Action provided by the arts motivates students to participate.

Uniting message and management

A strong message summary and a well-orchestrated development plan are the two key elements needed to deliver a solid lesson built around the arts. To ensure that the art activity successfully delivers the message, it is usually necessary to remind students as the lesson progresses of how the two tools—message and management—fit together.

Announcing that connection when you introduce the lesson is a good way to begin. Once students become engaged in the project, it is easy for them to lose track of the spiritual point that it is meant to exhibit. When you sense this shift in concentration, it's time to reenforce by restating the lesson's message and the way in which the project acts to teach it.

Finally, as part of your review or final prayer, use the finished arts project to remind students of the message you want them all to take home and share.

IS YOUR ARTS-CENTERED LESSSON A SUCCESS?

Teaching children about God by using the arts means relying on the arts as a primary tool to share a spiritual message. The success of such teaching, then, is not determined by the professional look or feel of the produced work.

You can compute the success of any art-centered lesson by answering questions like these.

- Did this lesson/project illustrate something essential about the nature of God or our relationship with God?

- Did the project demonstrate God's love, caring, and concern for creation?

- Were the children able to produce and recognize samples of the beauty of God's world?

- Were some of the unique ways in which God has gifted us revealed clearly?

- To what degree did this project raise or help to answer faith-centered questions for discussion?

■ Did students have an opportunity to learn from their own exploration and from the expressed perceptions of others?

Make sure to share these considerations with your students.

 *Questions*

Share with others or reflect by yourself on each of the following.

If you had a choice between using the arts or any other development approach, which would you choose and why?

For you, what is the most convincing argument for using the arts in the religious education classroom at least occasionally?

What do you foresee as the most difficult aspect of using an arts-centered project with the class of students you are currently teaching?

When was the last time you used an arts-related activity as part of lesson development? Did you consider this method a success? Why or why not?

How to review

At the end of most textbook chapters, you will find a section set aside and clearly marked "Review." In fact, you may see the word so routinely that it begins to lose its significance. When teaching time is tight, you may feel tempted to ignore the call to review. But as you discover why, when, and how to review, I hope you will come to agree that skipping the opportunity to review is seldom a sound teaching option.

WHY REVIEW?

Catechists' guides and DREs emphasize the importance of lesson reviews with good reason. They stand by their belief that reviewing is an essential part of every lesson for students and teachers alike.

Review: A student's tool

During class, students typically follow a learning path that first presents and then explores a grade-level topic related to God, the church, or the faith. While children are listening, reading, or participating in lesson activities, their minds wander down a half-dozen distracting trails—despite your best efforts and theirs. Not even the best student remains fully tuned in one hundred percent of the time.

Chapter reviews are presented at the end of most lessons to help students gather up and correctly reassemble the lesson's message, replanting it firmly in their minds before they leave class. To succeed, reviews are structured around the familiar and respected instructional tool—repetition.

The more opportunities there are for students to reconnect with the lesson's message, the greater the likelihood that students will retain its main features over the long term. Given the chance, most students will benefit from activities and exercises that revisit, repeat, or reenforce the chief points that make up the lesson's core.

While the primary goal of any review is learning through repetition, there are additional positive side effects to the practice. For students, the review opens the door for further discussion of a topic that is now somewhat familiar. Students who remain quiet when a topic is first presented may begin to feel comfortable enough during a review session to ask questions or offer observations that improve everyone's comprehension.

Participating in review activities leads students either to recognize and be pleased by their own success or to notice on their own that more attention to regular class work is in order. Either way, review provides students with a trustworthy framework for self- accountability.

Review: A catechist's tool

Lesson reviews are organized in ways that ask students to check their memory for the specifics of previous discussions, readings, or activities and then to share their recollection with the class and catechist.

When your class participates in a review, the results also serve you well by verifying the degree to which the lesson materials you shared were received by students. If, during review exercises, students respond swiftly with answers that show solid recall and good understanding, then you know you have hit the mark.

If, on the other hand, students seem surprised by review questions, look blankly into space, or offer answers that are shaky or disconnected from the topic, then you know you all have more work to do in this particular subject area.

Without a basic review, it can be too easy for you to assume that everyone has been listening, concepts have been absorbed, and the class is ready to move on. A review can reveal a very different scenario. The review is not so much a test of how good a teacher you are or how bright your students may be. The review is a helpful hurdle that keeps you from attempting to teach a new skill or idea before the previous one has been learned.

Moving on to the next topic prematurely can be damaging to the overall learning process because subject matter in most religion textbooks is presented sequentially. Topics are arranged in a predetermined order for maximum teaching success. If students skip over one step without thoroughly understanding its meaning, then the next step becomes more difficult to comprehend. The simple review guards you against moving on to teach about "the sacrament of baptism" when children are still unsure what is meant by the word "sacrament" or "baptism"; it keeps you from trying to teach the "Lord's Prayer" when the idea of "prayer" itself is still a mystery.

While surely not without its tedium, reviewing offers enough benefits for students to take it seriously and for teachers to include it in every lesson plan.

WHEN TO REVIEW

It's logical for you to presume that review always comes at the end of the lesson. But the truth is that a tool as valuable as the review—a tool that provides helpful feedback to both students and catechists—deserves more than one opportunity to perform. For that reason you may welcome the opportunity to use a form of review at three distinct junctures in each lesson.

1. Review as introduction

Catechists looking for a constructive method for opening a new lesson are well served by returning with the students to the last lesson covered. By linking aspects of the old lesson with concepts to be found in the new lesson, catechists produce a review tool that also serves as an effective introduction.

The weaving of related topics, past and present, offers children a comfortable approach to the day's lesson. Recognizing words and phrases from the previous week that sound familiar, they settle down quickly and confidently. How much easier it is for students to begin with the known and move to the unknown. How helpful it can be for you to have a few moments at the start of each lesson to address information gaps and evaluate the readiness of the class to move forward together.

Many catechists quickly attach to the idea of using a brief review as an introductory tool. Its regular use promotes a secure and reliable teaching rhythm for students and catechists.

2. Review as a catch-up

One of the most disappointing experiences for a volunteer catechist is to lead a lesson for almost sixty minutes only to discover at the end how very few of those who started out with you are still following along. This experience can and does happen with unfortunate frequency.

You can reverse the likelihood of losing students along the way by planning periodic pauses during the lesson for a mini-review. Done at the end of each major lesson sub-division and only lasting two or three minutes, the mini-review encourages kids to refocus, ask a question, take a breath, let the dust settle, benefit from someone else's question, or even pat themselves on the back because they are right on target.

For the teacher, the mini-review is a useful break in the "dash to the finish" approach that can become habit when there is lots of material to cover and seemingly too little time to cover it.

The text usually divides the full body of a lesson for you into several subdivisions. Paying attention to those divisions and holding just a very brief wrap-up at the conclusion of one or more will make a surprising contribution to your efforts to keep everyone together, on message, and retaining as they go.

3. Review as Summary

Of course, the customary spot to find the review is tacked to the end of the chapter. While the end of the lesson is certainly the optimum spot for a review, don't let its common position dictate its value. It's not just an add-on, a filler, or something to do if you have the time. Make no mistake: review is an essential element of a well-taught and comprehensible lesson.

Without some kind of brief review at lesson's end, what you have taught will tend to lack organization and closure. Instead of the structured unit you thought you prepared, the lesson can take on the feel of lots of unfinished and rather unrelated thoughts.

Students benefit from having a boundary drawn around what they are studying. The review responds to their need to reduce the sum total of what has been shared to a few meaningful, portable sentences. It furnishes a closing glimpse of what they have been talking about, what it all means, and how it all fits into the life they will reenter on the other side of the classroom door.

The review is not an extra. You and your students deserve all the benefits that can come from including a solid review in every lesson you share.

HOW TO REVIEW

Time set aside for review should, of course, be brief. Usually five minutes is sufficient for a review used to introduce a lesson, a couple of minutes for a mini-review during the lesson, and five to ten minutes for a final review. With so little time available, solid planning is key, especially for the final review.

Your catechist's guide includes review material for each chapter. But with the approval of your DRE, you may want to create your own lesson-specific alternatives. You might select one of the following formats for a successful end of lesson review.

- **Basic question and answer.** To individual students, pairs, or small groups, distribute a sheet with five basic questions related to the current chapter. Allow five minutes for students to construct a written or spoken response, and a few minutes to share responses in a full-group setting.

- **Three-word summary.** Give each child three individual file cards or slips of paper. Ask students to write the three most important words in the day's lesson, in large letters, writing one word on each card. Collect the cards, hold one up at a time, and ask students to volunteer definitions of each. Or alternately, write words from the cards on the board, and then beneath each word record how many students selected that same word. Talk about why the words with the most mentions were in fact so crucial to the lesson.

■ **Pictures tell the story.** Allot each child three crayons and a sheet of drawing paper. Ask them to produce a single drawing that in some way represents or is closely connected to the main theme of the day's lesson. Some pictures can be used by the teacher to help visually summarize the lesson. Others can be saved and used to review this week's lesson at the beginning of the lesson for next week.

■ **Mime your own business.** Ask students to work in threes to create a short miming sequence that effectively acts out all or any part of the message of the day's lesson without the use of words.

■ **What we served up.** Suggest students work in pairs to describe the day's lesson as if it were a meal appearing on a menu. Instruct students to list what part of the lesson was the main course, side dishes, dessert, and beverage. Share with the entire class.

■ **What you missed.** Direct students to use a folded sheet of paper and markers to design a simple card to be sent to a student who is absent. The center section of the card should offer a briefly worded summary of what happened during the lesson hour.

These formats are only samples of the many unique approaches catechists can create and use to accomplish the same end — the meaningful recall of the teaching message that you have just shared. Because of your very special knowledge of your own students, you will be able to tailor and implement reviews to meet both your teaching skills and their learning needs.

 *Questions*

Share with others or reflect by yourself on each of the following.

Imagine or recall from your own previous teaching experience reasons why you might occasionally decide to skip the closing review. Knowing the value of review, what steps could you take to avoid that situation in the future?

Which of the alternative review formats explained above appeals the most to you? Why is it a good fit for both you and your students?

Have you ever attempted a mid-lesson mini-review before? If yes, what results did it produce? If not, why not?

How to get the help you need

As a volunteer catechist, you routinely give your time, patience, caring, and teaching skills to help educate students in the faith. When occasionally your work as a catechist becomes a bit overwhelming, zero in on this truth: you are not meant to accomplish this task alone.

Remember that it is the entire parish family and the larger church community that are responsible for the religious training of young people. Your efforts, while important and appreciated, are but one part of a total parish effort. You can and should rely on more than just your own abilities and endurance to complete the grade-level work you have undertaken. But where do you turn to get help when you need it?

EVERYDAY HELP
Students, Catechists, and Catechist's Guide
Lots of assistance can be found almost at your fingertips. For example, for the most basic questions, you'll find immediate and reliable aid just by asking your students, especially those who have already spent a year in the program. Don't pass on

the chance to let them help you resolve your hunt for simple but essential items like the pencil sharpener, lavatory, or supply center. Most students welcome the opportunity to display their knowledge and are amazingly savvy in the ways of the classroom. You can also count on the support of experienced catechists teaching in adjacent rooms. They have stood where you are standing now and will be generous with their response. If you need direction about when the attendance cards get turned in, how to get additional texts, or how to close up the room when class is over, your catechist colleagues are there for you.

Don't overlook the catechist's guide you received before the year began. You already know that the guide contains weekly lesson plans. You can refer to the guide both before and during the lesson to stay on target and to accomplish the lesson goals. But there's more.

A deeper investigation reveals that many guides show you the way around your chosen grade level. Want to know more about likely student behavior patterns? Interested in discovering what your students should already know about the faith? Need some advice on the ideal teaching approach to use for your grade level? Your catechist's guide may be a good place to begin.

Such grade-specific teaching information is often found at the very beginning or end of the guide, but valuable nuggets are also tucked into individual lessons. Becoming familiar with how your guide is organized and what resources it contains can open the door to some worthwhile and easily accessible teaching advice.

The DRE

Not far away, possibly just down the hall, you may locate the volunteers' most frequently consulted "guide"—the DRE.

The role of the DRE is to smooth the teaching path for

volunteer catechists. Drawing upon her own unique training, teaching experiences, and skill set, the DRE is prepared to share approaches, methods, techniques, and resources to meet your classroom concerns.

What can you ask the DRE? Almost anything. In fact, many DREs would gladly hang out a shingle saying "No question too large or too small." They are enablers by trade, but they can't be successful at their job unless you make your needs clearly known.

Below are some examples of questions DREs readily and frequently field:

- How do I get more kids to participate?

- What do I do with repeat troublemakers?

- Should I contact this student's parents or will you?

- Is it okay to give homework?

- Can I show a movie next week? How do I get a TV monitor?

- Can I get an aide for the special-needs student in my class?

- I need a sub for the next two weeks. What do I do?

- I don't understand how to teach the Trinity. Can you help?

- Can I get some heat in my room? It's 45 degrees in there.

- What are the rules about cell phone use?

- What do I do with kids who read or write very slowly?

- Is there a nurse on duty or first aid kit I can use?

- Is it okay to dismiss my kids early if they have been really good?

■ One of the lavatory faucets won't turn off; what should I do?

You don't have to mull over these kinds of classroom problems and uncertainties. The presence of the DRE should be a constant reminder that you really aren't in this alone. The DRE represents the will of the parish to give you the support and the solutions you need as a catechist.

BEYOND EVERYDAY ISSUES

The majority of questions you need answered will arise out of ordinary classroom situations and standard lessons. But what if your concerns are less typical? What if the overall classroom format just isn't working for you? It might be that a change in your personal situation might cause you to miss half of your scheduled classes, or that the ins and outs of small-group or craft projects are just too much for you to manage, or that you feel unequal to the curriculum challenge posed by several upcoming lessons.

When the scope of the problem requires more than some marginal tweaking, it may be time to work with the DRE to fashion some large-scale, creative repairs like those discussed below.

Turn-teaching

The traditional classroom setting places the same individual catechist at the front of the same group of children each week throughout the teaching year. Sometimes the traditional way is simply not possible.

In those instances, your DRE may work with you to establish an arrangement to accomplish the same teaching ends. A partnership can be made up of two or even three volunteer catechists who alternate responsibility for classroom teaching according to a mutually agreeable schedule.

Volunteers who are not able to commit to teaching every

week can still serve as catechists, just with less frequency. This system of turn-teaching can reduce the pressure catechists experience when conflicts arise between their weekly teaching schedule and other work or family demands.

At the same time, turn-teaching means students have a chance to experience two or three different styles of teaching and faith role models on a rotating basis, which keeps lessons fresh and less predictable.

DREs are generally willing to foster a turn-teaching arrangement. With two or three people assuming responsibility for a rotating schedule, it will seldom be necessary for the DRE to call in a substitute to cover the class.

With the direction of the DRE and a few volunteers, you can turn-teach with the peace of mind that comes from being able to avoid conflicts by confidently scheduling your teaching absences ahead of time.

Team-teaching

Team-teaching is more than a change in the basic classroom format. Instead of one catechist leading the class, team-teaching suggests that there be a coordinated effort on the part of two or even three catechists to share a lesson with students.

In advance, team teachers organize the distribution of lesson sections to take advantage of each catechist's skills and avoid his or her weaknesses. From opening prayer to closing review, the team would proceed through the lesson, rotating leadership of activities according to each team member's abilities.

Team-teaching obviously requires a larger total number of teachers per class, but for each individual catechist, the teaching load becomes lighter and more comfortable. The total effect can be a more upbeat and more effectively taught class.

Not every turn- or team-teaching arrangement works

perfectly. Much of the success of either method rests on the ability of those involved to coordinate their efforts and take direction as needed from the DRE. Still, in situations where you are feeling stressed or current classroom management has become a weekly struggle, you should be aware there are workable alternatives to going it alone.

Parental Involvement

As a catechist, how often have you wished you had eyes in the back of your head or an extra set of hands? Certainly more than once.

Your dreams can almost come true. With the approval and help of your DRE, it may be possible for you to recruit extra classroom help from among the parents of your students. Not every parent will be willing or able to help out, but some will respond positively.

You are, of course, not asking parents to take on the role of a catechist. What you can search for are volunteers willing to tackle a pile of management chores currently owned by you. Volunteer parents bring with them those extra hands you were looking for. The assistance they provide may be as simple as passing out and collecting up project materials or spending time with a child who has been absent and needs help with some catch-up work. But whatever task they take on reduces your pile by one.

In fact, even if she or he doesn't pick up a piece of paper, the mere presence of a parent in almost any classroom is a plus. The parent supplies an extra adult awareness in the mix; those extra eyes you were looking for have arrived.

It's wonderful to invite parents in to participate in special projects, but from a catechist's point of view, any days on which you receive a bit of extra help are special by definition.

Teens, senior citizens, and parish family

Parents form a rather obvious assortment of potential helpers, but there are other sources of assistance that can be successfully tapped as well. Relying again on the support and advice of the DRE, why not investigate the possibility of teens joining you from time to time?

In addition to their keen intelligence, irrepressible humor, and instinctive kindness, teens know things about the culture of children that adults don't. They are close enough in age to children in your classes to understand them and communicate with them on an entirely different plane than you can. The rapport that they strike easily converts to a highly efficient teaching and managing tool you will welcome into the classroom

Senior citizens can enjoy the chance to lend you a hand in the classroom. They bring the unbeatable advantage in many cases of having grandchildren, grandnieces, or grandnephews of their own. They may be more comfortable with your students than you would have imagined.

Because many children have good relationships with their grandparents, they often react respectfully and connect well to seniors. Sometimes better than grown-ups, children seem intuitively to recognize the strengths and limitations of seniors and engage with them accordingly.

And what about those folks who don't have children in the program and aren't seniors or teens but have a bit of time to share? There really are parishioners who are terrified by the prospect of teaching, but who wouldn't mind serving the parish as an occasional helper. Some may even turn out to be specialists, folks who can play a mean guitar, dazzle on a computer, or know their way around a stage. If you know such a person, pass the name to your DRE, and together you may gather up a new recruit.

Of course, there is more to getting extra help than just corralling well-intentioned people. With the direction of your DRE, you can give assistants the advanced notice, solid direction, and age-appropriate tasks that can help ensure an enjoyable and productive relationship.

Because you have prepared well to become a catechist, you may be surprised when confronted with daily problems or the need for format changes that you never anticipated. Don't struggle on alone. Recognize that you and your class stand to benefit from your willingness to search out parish resources from students to senior citizens. Go ahead: draw upon and be empowered by the spiritual community around you. Religious education is a parish responsibility.

 *Questions*

Share with others or reflect by yourself on each of the following.

Can you share an example of a time when as a catechist you sought help? What did you need? Whom did you ask? How helpful was their response?

Do you think generally you are more likely to need help with the teaching message or the management/development of a lesson? Explain your choice.

If you had to choose, which teaching alteration would you prefer—turn-teaching or team-teaching? Why?

To which group (parents, teens, seniors, other parishioners) would you look first in selecting a part-time, in-room helper? Why?

How to discipline

You like working with children, and you are a person of faith. Still, when you think about how to get and hold the attention of children long enough to share the faith, you sometimes feel helpless and hopeless. For you and many other volunteers, disciplining students may well be the least appealing, most challenging aspect of serving as a catechist.

Unfortunately, every classroom activity, done by individuals or in groups, from the opening prayer to the wrap-up review, relies for success on the backdrop of a well-managed classroom. There just really is no way around it. Knowing how to discipline is a must.

WHERE TO BEGIN

The cornerstone to an orderly, productive classroom is the establishment of an environment in which disciplinary encounters seldom occur and the need to apply rules all but vanishes. As you might suspect, building that kind of learning-friendly atmosphere is an ongoing task and one that begins immediately.

At the very first meeting, you can frame acceptable classroom behaviors by sharing a few basic in-class procedures. For instance, children need to know from the start when they are permitted to do things like sharpen a pencil, chat freely, use the restroom, or line up for dismissal. Addressing such concerns up front will reduce both the number of student questions and potential disruption.

You'll also want to explain your set of disciplinary expectations. Calling on students to model their behavior according to Christ's law of love is both solid ground and a requirement children of all ages can understand. You are simply calling upon everyone to recognize that no matter how old, smart, pretty, funny, athletic, crafty, or musical we might be, Jesus calls upon us all to follow the same two rules: Love God and love neighbor.

When we love God and our neighbor (everyone), then we make a consistent effort to avoid evil and destructive or unkind thoughts, words, and actions. In the classroom, love for God and neighbor means we are kind, considerate, and helpful, that we don't bully others by what we say or do, that we talk in turn when we are called upon, and that we all do our very best to respect one another.

Focusing and refocusing children on the need to care for and respect their classmates and their catechist can provide a calming and corrective effect and a protected space for teaching and learning.

BUILDING A PRODUCTIVE CLASSROOM ENVIRONMENT

With Jesus' law of love in place, you can take up the ongoing process of forging a constructive learning atmosphere. Recognize the truth that in the end it is the way in which you teach, each and every week, supported by the law of love, that will create a dependable environment for sharing the faith.

Recalling the suggestions of chapters written here can help you piece together well-taught, quality lessons. Collectively, the ways in which you present those lessons form your response to the catechist's ultimate challenge: teaching a classroom of busy, active, sometimes hard to corral, children.

Consider the subtle disciplinary effects produced in each of these teaching scenarios.

When you teach well for sixty minutes

Catechists who come to class ready to teach well for sixty minutes give themselves a clear-cut advantage. When you arrive knowing where you're going (message) and how you're going to get there (management), you put yourself in a take-charge posture before students even arrive.

By fully orienting yourself to your lesson, you give yourself the precious gift of confidence. As you open each lesson, you send out the clear, straightforward message that you are a catechist who is in charge and on a mission. More often than not, your confidence encourages students to stay tuned to see what happens next.

As the lesson proceeds, children will pick up on stand-out aspects of your teaching style. You definitely have a message you want to share. You conscientiously stay on that message and stick to your own time schedule. Students note that while you welcome their questions, you're not easily distracted. They respect how smoothly you draw the class to its timely completion.

Because of your preparation, there is no confusion at the front of the room, no searching for ideas, equipment, or clues about how to proceed. Students may know that you are not a professional teacher, but by the end of sixty minutes they are also convinced that you are a well-prepared catechist. Your pleasant but no-nonsense approach gives students a sense of comfort and security in the classroom.

From the students' point of view, there is more good news. During your first hour together they sensed your willingness to share "with" them rather than teach "at" them. They felt that way because when you saw puzzled looks, you didn't just charge ahead with the text; you took time to translate the unfamiliar into the familiar so that everyone could move on together.

You made the lesson more human. You didn't go on all day about your own experiences, but you weren't afraid to share, especially when your sharing opened the door for them to share as well.

When students encounter a well-prepared, well-organized catechist obviously dedicated to bringing an important message home to them, generally they think twice before choosing to cause a problem.

When you motivate students

You know that idle minds, unfocused minutes, and disconnected feelings are indeed the devil's playground. You also know that you can't eliminate those potentially negative elements from your classroom simply with a list of rules. You opt for a more successful approach. You determine to motivate students.

You act on the belief that when idle minds are stirred by action, unfocused minds are centered by interesting objects, and disconnected thoughts are reassembled around personal interests, then overall attention problems are significantly reduced, students get involved, and good things begin to happen.

That's why you seldom come to class without a focus item or two to spark student attention. It explains the care you take to include learning activities that allow students time to move or talk or both. It's the reason you consistently highlight spots in your lesson plan that you can effectively link to known student interests.

Making use of motivational tools that improve focus, inspire action, and trigger a personal connection is your way of using positive means to achieve disciplinary ends. By acknowledging basic student needs for focus, motion, and connection as you plan, you have made the lesson accessible and user friendly. It may sound contradictory, but you've found that a sure route to rein kids in is to help kids open up.

When you use small-group activities

Employing small-group activities definitely represents a change in basic classroom management. Instead of teaching from the front of the room, you actively funnel the teaching message via student groups and an accompanying instruction sheet.

Teaching through small groups has required you to prepare more, but in return you find that your workload during the class hour has become considerably less. The activities you offer provide student groups a message focus, connect them in a personal way to the lesson, and, best of all, provide lots of options for motion that empowers.

Some might question the extension of liberties that come with small-group activities. Your experience tells you that it is precisely this kind of open participation that eliminates classroom boredom and addresses students' pent-up need for action.

When you use small-group activities, you signal your willingness and determination to channel excess student energy away from inappropriate actions to the pursuit of spiritually enriching projects—often without raising your voice or even an eyebrow.

When you teach with the arts

You've discovered that the arts are much more than just an escape from the textbook for you and the class. Art forms provide everyone with an exciting way to alternate learning approaches and open the door for the free flow of ideas and perceptions.

Well-organized, well-supervised arts-related projects focus children in such a way as to maintain order throughout the room and the hour while turning individual minds loose to wander and create.

You make it a point not to make the arts boring by over-scheduling their use. But you don't avoid them either. By alternating the use of the arts with various other teaching tools, you can almost guarantee that when it comes time for some arts-centered teaching, kids will be cheerful, attentive, and ready to connect with God in their own special way. Little coaxing is required.

When you review

There are predictable times within the teaching hour when there is a potential for discipline issues to arise:

- At the beginning of class when students are reluctant to settle down and begin

- Midway through the class, as time begins to weigh heavily, especially on age groups with limited attention spans

- At the end of class when everyone's patience is running thin and the clock is visibly ticking toward dismissal

When those situations arise, your motto becomes "don't grab a rule, grab a tool." Your personal favorite in such situations is review activities. The regular use of varied review exercises encourages kids to reset by taking a second, more relaxed look at a previously examined topic. For you and your students, review time, whenever it is inserted, acts as a welcome decompressor.

When you get the help you need

Starting a class knowing there are pieces missing in your preparation could cause you to be anxious and irritable and to upset your otherwise attentive classroom. Sensing you're out of sorts, students could become less cooperative, failing to keep their own emotions and behaviors in check. Dragging out a classroom rule isn't going to mend that kind of situation. Getting the help you need will. That's why you make sure to tie up all the loose ends of any lesson well before class begins.

To avoid last minute disarray, you check days ahead with the DRE when you need help with lesson content. You phone some volunteers who might monitor the skits you've planned. You organize a scheme for quickly cleaning and resetting the room before the end of class. It all takes time, but the dividends are obvious when you come in to class ready to roll and you find students ready to roll right along with you.

Supplementing your own skills, knowledge, and classroom awareness through the help of others, especially on busy days, or choosing to use turn- or team-teaching arrangements are in themselves statements of your commitment to maintain an orderly classroom. The presence of additional adult assistance is not lost on children. They get the message loud and clear without any explanation: nothing is going through the cracks here; the law of love and good behavior will continue to be the norm for the day, no need for discussion.

BUT WHAT IF?

Your commitment to employing Jesus' firm but gentle law

of love and your consistent efforts to teach well-planned lessons offer a reliable plan for creating and maintaining discipline as you share the faith. Minor disciplinary actions, when needed, will most often center around reminding one or more students about the classroom expectation that everyone treats others with kindness, care, respect, and Christian love.

But what happens when the reintroduction of the law of love or sharpening up your lesson preparation doesn't produce the results you want? Suppose a student is openly disrespectful, consistently disruptive, or willfully belligerent in the classroom? What then?

It is likely that at the beginning of the teaching year the DRE will provide you with procedures for managing such unpleasantness. They are likely to include reasonable steps like those below.

- Make a preliminary attempt to resolve the issue by speaking privately with the student(s) to clarify exactly what the law of love requires of him or her. Concentrate on the word "respect" and its meaning in relationships in the classroom, making certain that the student understands what changes in behavior he or she needs to put in motion.

- Attempt to get agreement from the student that his or her behavior will be promptly altered. Explain what consequences will follow if improvement is not made immediately, and promise that you will deliver on those consequences.

- Often such a serious, firm, one-on-one discussion is sufficient to bring the student into line because you will be heard as one speaking from a position of well-established authority.

- Make the DRE aware of the conversation. She may suggest other alternatives to follow at this juncture.

- If the unacceptable action continues, waste no time in bringing the student's behavior, or the student, to the attention of the DRE by whatever means the program director has suggested.

- Whenever in doubt, rely on the available disciplinary backup provided by the DRE.

- It is seldom the responsibility of volunteer teachers to engage parents in discussions of student misbehavior. Those conversations are territory usually reserved to the DRE.

- Move on. Continue to do the best teaching job you can and to work with all students to model Jesus' commandment to love.

DISCIPLINE—TOOL OF TOOLS

Discipline is a unique teaching tool. It both comes from and contributes to solid teaching experiences. From one perspective, discipline is a result of the way in which you plan and deliver each lesson. Seen from another viewpoint, discipline provides the essential backdrop for the productive use of every other teaching tool you use. What is certain is that discipline enhances and protects a teaching space in which you can do the job you signed on to complete.

Looking at a classroom full of bubbly, rambunctious children, it's easy to feel the odds for success are stacked against you. To the degree that you lean on Jesus' law of love, share solid lessons geared to your students, and rely on the professional support of your DRE, you can begin each class with a smile, knowing you are more than equal to the task.

 *Questions*

Share with others or reflect by yourself on each of the following.

Can you remember a teacher from your own past who disciplined at least in part using Jesus' law of love? How did you and your classmates react to that approach?

What does the author mean when she suggests that "discipline provides the essential backdrop for the productive use of every other teaching tool you use"? Explain why you agree or disagree.

What other factors besides the law of love and sound teaching habits do you think might add to the creation of a well-disciplined classroom?

For you what is the most taxing part of the teaching hour? Beginning, mid-point, ending, or other? Can you explain why?

How to evaluate
your teaching

It really doesn't matter whether you served up a new recipe, ran a half-marathon, or bought a birthday present for a friend. Our human nature nudges us to measure the success of our efforts. Having dedicated the time and energy needed to prepare a lesson and deliver it to a group of children, you want and deserve feedback. By evaluating your performance, you not only satisfy your curiosity; you take prompt and effective action toward growing as a catechist.

To produce results that are both fair and meaningful, you may wish to frame your evaluation around four defining questions:

- When should evaluation be done?

- What aspects of your teaching should be evaluated?

- Who should do the evaluating?

- What should you do with what you learn?

WHEN SHOULD EVALUATION BE DONE?
Reviewing how you teach is obviously an essential and ongoing process. The sooner you attempt some very basic evalua-

tion, the sooner you can take steps to improve your methods and the results of your teaching. Continuing some form of evaluation throughout the year will ensure that you continue to grow and develop as a secure catechist

Same-week evaluation

In the hours after dismissing your first class, your mind may still be a jumble filled with a confused collection of impressions and concerns. It's certainly not the best time to rush to judgment. To make the best sense out of your first teaching experience, let the dust settle. Wait a day or two, grab a few quiet minutes, and then very briefly jot down what stands out in your mind about that first teaching event.

While your intention may well be to itemize everything you believe you did wrong and fix it all before you appear for the next class, you'll have better results if you limit your evaluation to one key question. After sixty minutes in the classroom, did you feel like you had shared the central message of the first lesson or not? All the other questions—how the kids responded, how you reacted to the students, how this or that technique did or didn't live up to expectations—are important but secondary aspects that can be taken up one by one as the year progresses.

All you really need to know at the start is: were you successful in transmitting the message from the book to the students? If the answer is "yes," you are off to a positive beginning. Plan to stick with the approach that worked and gradually build on it in the weeks to come.

If you were less than satisfied with your first teaching experience, then consider what happened that kept you from a satisfactory sharing of the message. Give consideration to these possible problems.

- Was unsure of the message from the beginning
- Spent too much time getting started and never quite regrouped, so the lesson message was rushed
- Got thrown off message throughout the lesson because of disruptive students and distracting questions
- Had difficulty using the main teaching tool suggested by the text
- Lacked a good end of class review that might have pulled things together

Talking through the stalling points of your lesson with an experienced teacher or the DRE can help you to improve your second attempt.

Continuing this kind of mini-evaluation each week, asking yourself if you delivered the message or not (and if not, then why not), will help you to target and correct teaching problems. Sticking to this regular schedule of personal evaluation is a sure way to arrest problems before they take root in your classroom. Ignoring the need to evaluate and address difficulties is not a solution.

Half-year evaluation. Before returning to class after the Christmas holidays, your DRE may suggest, or you may request, the opportunity to talk through how you are progressing. Keeping yourself accountable on a regular weekly basis will go a long way toward reducing some problems and clarifying others, thus making a mid-year evaluation a simple, straightforward undertaking.

Even if it only lasts for fifteen minutes, that time spent with the DRE should not be time wasted. Talking through needed or suggested changes in approach at this juncture will allow you to go back into the classroom renewed, encouraged, and prepped for a fresh start.

End-of-year evaluation. Looking back over the course of twenty-five weeks or so of completed class activities may seem rather pointless. Even if you plan to teach next year, do you really need to go through more paperwork now?

If nothing else, end-of-the-year evaluations can give you a sense of closure rather than confusion as the teaching season ends. Comparing your teaching from the beginning of the year to the end can give you a sense of pride and bolster your enthusiasm to return.

The end-of-the-year evaluation is also the prime time to stock up on DRE suggestions. Notes you take at the end of the year—your own or those provided by the DRE—can make things much easier should you choose to volunteer again.

There is very little that is more helpful for teachers returning in the fall than being able to take a look at evaluations from the previous year. Don't cheat yourself out of this help by skipping that final evaluation.

WHAT ASPECTS OF YOUR TEACHING SHOULD BE EVALUATED?

Evaluations open up thinking and discussion about everything that takes place in the classroom. To prompt those open thoughts or chats, you might choose to center on one or more of these topics:

Have you shared the message?

The role of the catechist is to share the faith. When you begin to evaluate your teaching experience, all discussion really needs to begin with and revolve around the single question: how well did you share the message?

Have you successfully employed management tools?

As the topic of sharing the message plays out, you will undoubtedly come upon a second crucial question tightly bound to the first: how well have you used management tools?

You'll want to review to what degree your success or failure in sharing the message was connected to the way in which you were able to use the various suggested teaching techniques. What were the difficulties you encountered? What other teaching options might have worked better for you?

Have you met initial expectations?

A useful evaluation grid can develop from reconsidering how well you have fulfilled the expectations held by parents, teachers, and students at the outset of the year (and noted in Chapter 1 of this book). To what degree did you

- Have a plan

- Value each child

- Teach at grade level

- Discipline

- Model the faith

- Be yourself

WHO SHOULD DO THE EVALUATING?

Students: There are those who would dispute or even ignore the value of student opinion about the teaching ability of catechists. They would suggest that students are fickle and their assessments unreliable. Too often, they would argue, students place more emphasis on their catechist being pleasant and easy-going, rather than on her or him being an effective teacher of the faith.

Keeping in mind the limitations of student judgment, there is still something important to be gained by surveying student opinion, especially through the medium of well-framed, direct questions. It is the students, after all, who are actually present and observing one hundred percent of what takes place in the classroom. It is the students who are most impacted by the quality of the teaching they receive. Their opinions, when carefully extracted, deserve to be heard.

DRE: In carrying out thorough and serviceable evaluations, the Director of Religious Education is at once the least and the most reliable judge of your abilities. Least, because he or she, by necessity, has only witnessed a small fraction of what you have done or not done as a catechist. Most, because he or she sees and hears with experienced eyes and ears. Even with only marginal exposure to your teaching style, there is still an excellent likelihood that very early on in the teaching year the DRE will have good insight into the strengths and shortcomings you demonstrate.

You: Certainly the most prejudiced evaluator of all, you have the inside track of being present through all of your teaching, but also of seeing and hearing yourself from a totally biased perspective. The result can be that, because you lack experience, you are uncertain about how aspects of your teaching are being received. You have an opinion, but you really need to rely on the findings—both positive and negative—from student and DRE observations.

Evaluation is a ticklish matter. It is very difficult to get a totally reliable picture from anyone. That's why it's important to hear everyone out and then make sensible deductions from all collected opinions, with the direction of the DRE.

WHAT SHOULD YOU DO WITH WHAT YOU LEARN?

Evaluations have the potential to reveal causes and suggest solutions to teaching problems. They stand to be of greatest value if, in applying them, you keep in mind the following:

- Willingly open yourself to the critical judgments of all, but don't jump to amend your style without the guidance of the DRE; and then make changes gradually.

- Take comfort in knowing that every catechist, new or experienced, has teaching shortcomings. Don't let concern about your weaknesses overshadow joy in your many strengths.

- Believe that, like every volunteer catechist, you have the potential to develop and grow through training and experience.

- Relax in the sure knowledge that, while you may have learned much in a single year about HOW to teach, much more is left to be discovered.

- No one is ever quite finished with improving, but together we all work toward God's greater glory.

 *Questions*

Share with others or reflect by yourself on each of the following.

Can you recall situations or positions in which you have been evaluated? Who did the evaluating? How helpful was the process?

How valuable do you think your students' opinions about your teaching might be? What one question about your teaching would you like to ask members of your current class?

Are you likely to evaluate your teaching on a weekly basis? Why or why not?

To which of the expectations from the beginning of the year do you think you have responded most effectively? Least effectively?